Life of Riley

"Tails" of a treasured life!

by

Chris Rosinski
(with lots of help from Riley)

AuthorHouse™
1663 Liberty Drive
Bloomington, IN 47403
www.authorhouse.com
Phone: 1-800-839-8640

© 2010 Chris Rosinski (with lots of help from Riley). All rights reserved.

No part of this book may be reproduced, stored in a retrieval system, or transmitted by any means without the written permission of the author.

First published by AuthorHouse 5/14/2010

ISBN: 978-1-4490-9710-3 (SC)

Library of Congress Control Number: 2010903447

Printed in the United States of America
Bloomington, Indiana

This book is printed on acid-free paper.

Dedicated to every dog that ever touched a human heart!!

August 2013

Linda & Greg -

I understand the two of you love dogs as much as my husband & I do!

Happy Reading!
CHRIS Rosinski

(P.S. Give Jack & Ditto a hug for me!)

PROLOGUE

January 12, 1997

Miss Riley (a 10 week old Brittany/Irish Setter mix) came into our lives the day following a cruise vacation. We were mourning the loss of one of our four-legged girls and needed a puppy to fill the void.

After spending a great deal of time deciding (well, really it was Dad) we decided on our girl. I always knew her name would be Riley and the name suited her so well. Her big sister, Shyloe, a moody big Irish Setter, handled the new little life rather well.

We so enjoyed the new bundle of energy, especially since she was our first puppy as a couple. Little did we know the happiness, laughter, fears, tears and pain all of us would endure throughout her treasured life.

LIFE OF RILEY

January 12, 1997

I sure was lucky when that big man (Dad) spent so much time picking me out. I had no idea that I would have the most special life of any dog on earth. I won him over when I pressed my face up against his face and hugged him.

My first day home with my new Mom!

January 14, 1997

I weighed in at 12 lbs. today and leaped off the back porch and my big sister, Shyloe, took her first nip at me - but I came back for more! I had my first bath and I was not happy about it at all!

January 16, 1997

I jumped off Mom & Dad's big bed tonight when Mom got home from a meeting. Mom was rather proud of me!

January 18, 1997

I had my first trip to the vet today. Mom said I was a very good girl. I guess I almost fell asleep on the table. Then Mom took me to her hair salon to show me off and we found out that one of the girls that works there has one of my brothers - what a small world!

Now, off to Grandpa & Grandma's - I won them over! I slept on Mom's winter coat on the kitchen floor and they loved me. Grandpa made some comment about me being a girl and having a boy name - but, he still liked me!

January 31, 1997

I really like the big bed Mom & Dad sleep in - I would rather spend the day there than in that crate they call a "fort."

This is what my dog Mom looks like!!

February, 1997
___

My big sister is really starting to like me. We play outside and she takes me on adventures around a big pond.

Here is a picture of Shyloe.

February 22, 1997

I went back to the vet and gained 3 lbs. I got another shot in the neck - I hear that there are more to come!

I am starting to give my Mom a hard time in the morning - I promise her that I will be good if I can just stay under the bed all day.

March, 1997

My big sister only makes me cry about once a week now. Shyloe and I chase each other around the house and play - I really think she likes me!

I finally figured out how to jump up into the big bed - I am so proud of myself!

March 28, 1997

I went to the vet and got my last booster and rabies shot - I didn't like it at all this time. I cried and the vet (Dr. K) felt real bad. Mom made my appointment to get my tubes tied in three weeks.

April 18, 1997

I went to the hospital today to get my tubes tied (that is so I won't have puppies.) Mom dropped me off and neither one of us cried. Dr. Kim called at 12:00 to let Mom & Dad know that I was out of surgery and doing fine.

April 19, 1997

Mom picked me up right at 9:30 to bring me home. I wasn't myself and I threw up and peed in the car. Dad didn't even get mad at me when I did it because he loves me so much. I was pretty quiet all day - my tummy hurt and I didn't like jumping off the bed.

April 26, 1997

Mom took me to the vet clinic to get my stitches out. I hung on real tight to Dr. K. and he clipped them out. I'm all back to normal now!

This picture was taken when I was only about five months old.

May, 1997

Mom, Dad and Shyloe took me on my first camping trip to Canada. Boy, did we have fun! Mom & Dad weren't very smart - they made my leash out of nylon and when they weren't looking, I chewed the leash off of my collar and decided to do some sniffing.

Camping dinners are the best!

July, 1997

Mom, Dad and Shyloe took me on our boat for the first time. I had my own life jacket.

Summer, 1997

These guys (my family) show me some cool stuff. We go camping and boating - it is like being a real kid!

October, 1997

My Mom had to have surgery so she was home for a month and Shyloe and I loved it. We didn't have to go in our forts and it was so cool!

November 5, 1997

I turned 1 today. Mom made me a special treat!

December, 1997

I had my first Christmas and I had my own stocking with my name on it - it was great!

February 18, 1998

It was a terrible day! I got hit by a car and I didn't like it very much! My Dad let me out when he got home from work and I ran across the street. When my Mom got home she took me to see Dr. K. and he x-rayed me because I was coughing, but nothing was broken. They had to give me some medicine to bring me out of shock. I was really sore and scared for a few days. Of course, Mom took real good care of me.

Spring, 1998

My Mom and Dad took me to the vet with Shyloe today. Shyloe was in a lot of pain because she hurt her back. I thought I was going to lose my big sister today. Dr. Kim gave her some medicine to help her feel better.

Mom weighed me since I was at the clinic and I weighed 54 lbs. - only 4 lbs. less than my big sister (Mom thinks I'm getting fat!!)

Summer, 1998

I learned all about catching baby rabbits and birds. Dad gets really mad at me but I can't help it!!

Shyloe and I spent the summer swimming in Fisher Bay and running on the beach at Seaway Island. I am exhausted after all that activity!

August, 1998

Mom and Dad bought Shyloe and me a cottage in Canada on Lake Huron. It is so great! I have a lake in my front yard and a farm in my back yard. There are two little girls who just love to come and visit us all the time.

September, 1998

My Mom had to have surgery again and had to leave me and Shyloe for a few days. I think she was more upset about it than us. Dad took us to the cottage until she came home. She stayed home from work a long time and we really spoiled her - well, actually she spoiled us - but don't tell anyone because we were supposed to be taking care of her.

November, 1998

My Mom went back to work so that meant Shyloe and I had to go back in our forts during the day. I wish Shyloe wasn't afraid of stuff - this fort stuff is no fun! We just heard that our Dad is going to be home for awhile - yes, no more forts!!

Winter, 1999

My Mom and Dad take us to the cottage and we play in the snow and walk on the beach.

Spring, 1999

Mom bought me a collar that has paw prints on it and it glows in the dark. Now she can tell where I'm at in bed!

Shyloe got locked in Mr. Judd's garage and Mom, Dad and me couldn't find her for hours. We looked and looked and looked but couldn't find her. We thought she had either gotten lost or died and Dad was real upset. I think he thought he was in trouble with Mom because he was supposed to be watching us. We finally found her about 9:00 at night when she started barking. I ran to the garage door with Thor (our neighbor poodle friend) and we both were so happy that she was still alive. Only one problem, Mr. Judd wasn't home and we couldn't get her out. Mr. Judd's daughter came over with a key and finally let her out.

Summer, 1999

We spent the whole summer playing on the beach at the cottage. It is so much fun there! I learned how to catch fish!

We have lots of friends at Setter Ridge - that is what my Mom & Dad call the cottage - you know they really like us and wanted to name the cottage after us. Doogie, Milton, Chaucer, Rufus and Tia all come to visit us as soon as we get there.

January 4, 2000

Grandpa Fetterly passed away today and went to heaven. Mom & Dad feel real bad. Shyloe and I can tell they are hurting. Mom needs lots of kisses right now. We are taking real good care of her. We snuggle in bed with her and take her for long walks.

January 28, 2000

I don't know what happened to me today but I got real sick and had dizzy spells. I was home with Shyloe and Dad and he was real scared. He put me in the car and took me to the vet. He called Mom and she met us there. I was real nervous - and I really don't like going to that place. The Dr. checked me over and thought everything was okay, but wanted to keep me for a few hours to keep an eye on me. Mom & Dad had to leave me - we were all real sad. They shaved my leg and put a needle in it - I licked it to make it feel better. Shyloe was real lonely at home by herself - she really does love me!

Mom, Dad and Shyloe came to pick me up and Dad brought Miss Kitty (my stuffed animal) for me. The Dr. said they couldn't find anything wrong with me - they also said I needed to go on a diet!! Mom & Dad have been real good about not feeding me junk food - I should be skinny by this summer!

Spring/Summer, 2000

We had lots of fun at Setter Ridge this summer. I love looking for fish in Lake Huron. Shyloe is getting old and she has trouble climbing the stairs, but she won't give up so I wait for her so we can climb them together.

Mom & Dad decided we needed a new house so they have been real busy working on the new house all summer.

December, 2000

We moved in to our new house during a snowstorm. At first, Shyloe and I were kind of scared and nervous but we finally got used to it. We even have a fence so we can stay outside all the time. I already have a bunny to tease!

Spring/Summer, 2001

We feel like we have been at our new house forever. Mom & Dad take us for walks to the park and we run and smell bunnies and deer. I get so excited when they tell us we are going that I jump in the air like a kangaroo.

We have dog neighbors, Comet and Lasher. They are real nice and I like them a lot.

My Mom got tired of always checking on us at the cottage, so we got a fence there too. It is great, I get to go outside all the time!

For some reason, I keep getting those dizzy spells and I don't like them. When I know that I am going to have one, I run to my Mom so she can hold me. My Dad is real good with taking care of me when I'm trembling - I think he loves me lots!

July 21, 2001

Shyloe went to heaven today. We didn't think it was going to be this summer but she was getting real tired. Mom knew when it was time and she told Dad and me that we needed to say goodbye to Shyloe. It was real sad - but we didn't want her to be in pain. She was almost 14 and Mom & Dad had spoiled her rotten.

I'm trying to be happy without my big sister - but I'm not sure yet. Mom & Dad said if I'm real lonely I can have a new sister. All I have to do is tell them and they will get another four-legged red girl.

September-December, 2001

I've kind of had a rough time since my big sister went to heaven. After missing her for a few weeks I got used to being alone during the day when Mom & Dad are at work. They really spoil me now that I'm the "only child."

I got sick Labor Day weekend and had to go to the Dr.'s a couple of times. I ate something I wasn't supposed to and I was in real bad shape for about a week. Then, in November, I ate too much pork (I love pork!!) and I got a really bad tummy ache. I got so nervous being at the vet clinic that I had one of those darn dizzy spells again.

I have a big bump on my leg that Mom & Dad are worried about. Dr. Mark said it had to come off right away. So, on Nov. 30th I had to go to the hospital again and have surgery. I was okay and they gave me a hot pink cast to keep my leg warm and safe.

Here I am when I had surgery - I wasn't very happy but Mom & Dad said it would be okay.

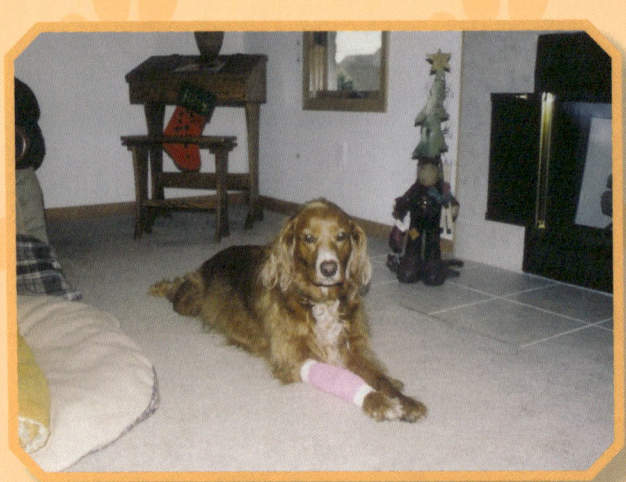

We went to look at a new sister for me, but she was crazy. She made me nervous and jealous. I really don't want to share my Mom & Dad (or my food) with another four legged sibling. I think Mom & Dad maybe want another red dog, but they worry about me so they didn't bring that crazy girl home. That is why I love them so much!

January, 2002

I've made lots of friends at the park - Corey (he is old and reminds me of Shyloe) and then there are Brutus and Ollie - all the boys like me!

I did get chewed up by two girls in the park the other day. I wasn't doing anything wrong so I don't know what their problem was. I cried and cried, and as usual, Mom & Dad made it all better. Mom even went to their house and told on them - she was not happy!!

One Saturday morning Mom took me for a walk in the woods and we saw a coyote. Mom was afraid he was going to chew me up!

October, 2002

We had lots of fun with the kids in the neighborhood on Halloween. Mom and me made special treats for the kids that play with me. I only barked at one little girl - she was dressed up like a cat and I couldn't help myself - I thought she was a real cat!!

I even had a costume - Mom took pictures - I'm sure she will put them in my photo gallery.

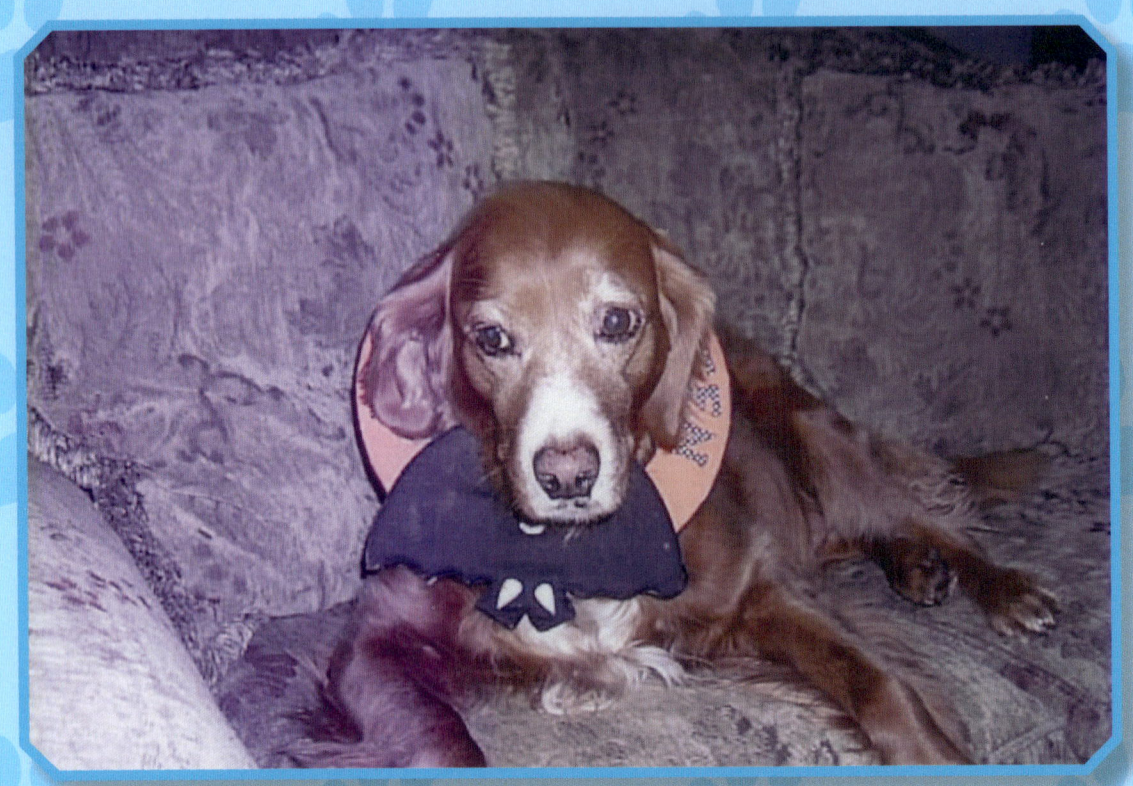

November, 2002

I've decided that I really like sleeping in Mom & Dad's big bed. Every night when I get tired, I tell Mom & Dad that I want to go to bed and Mom puts me in! Most nights I crawl under the bed for a few minutes. Dad thinks I go down there to say my prayers.

It doesn't take very long and Mom & Dad miss me and they sing a song to get me to come back to bed. They sing, "Riley Butt, Riley Butt where are you - Riley Butt, Riley Butt we love you!" They are crazy about me!

February, 2003

This time Dad had to have surgery to have a big bump taken out of him - just like the one I had on my leg. I took very good care of him. We laid on the couch together and I made sure he was safe. He told me that I did a better job of taking care of him than Mom!

Spring is just around the corner and pretty soon we will be going to the cottage - I can't wait!

Dad took this picture of me and Mom - it is my favorite picture of my Mom.

Summer, 2003

We had a great time at the cottage. Mom and me spent lots of time there by ourselves. We took lots of walks and I caught lots of fish.

I've been real good about not getting my dizzy spells. I think a lot of it has to do with Mom's nerves - we figured out that when she is stressed I get upset!

Ollie has become more like my stepbrother than my boyfriend. His Mom, Connie, who is a real nice lady comes and picks us up after work and we go to the park. Of course, I ride in the front with Connie and Mom sits in the back with Ollie.

Halloween, 2003

We had another great Halloween - Mom dressed up like a cat and I dressed up like a dog - which wasn't very hard to do!!

Here is a picture of the two of us.

November 5, 2003

Here I am on my 7th birthday. Of course, Mom & Dad made a big deal about it.

December, 2003

I gave Mom & Dad a real scare the other night. Mom let me out in the middle of the night and I saw a bunny or a cat and found out the gate wasn't shut. So, I took off down the street after the critter. Well, Mom thought someone had stolen me and she called the police (911.) They didn't get very excited that I was missing and they told Mom that 911 wasn't really for reporting lost dogs. Needless to say, Mom was not happy with the 911 people!

I finally came home after I heard Mom screaming for me. Dad was real upset too - you know, I am his "pride and joy."

Here is a picture of me and Dad having "quality time" together at the cottage.

Mom gave me and Dad a new dog for Christmas. She made her and she is stuffed and doesn't bark. Mom named her Nutmeg. I didn't like her at first - I thought she was real and I was going to have to share my parents and food with her. Now, she is my buddy - I grab her and take her in the van with me when we go to the cottage.

April, 2004

The only bad thing about being the only child is Mom makes me do stuff that I don't think she made the other girls do. She took me to a hair salon and they gave me a bath and cut and blew my hair dry. I wasn't very happy about the whole thing. I did look very cute and Mom & Dad got lots of compliments.

I'm afraid this is going to become a regular thing. Check out the bows in my ears!

Spring, 2004

This is me and Ollie. He has a bad knee and hip and we can't walk with him and Connie right now. We really miss our daily runs in the woods. Ollie taught me how to kind of climb a tree and catch Mr. Squirrel.

Here I am going after Mr. Squirrel - Ollie is so proud of me!

Summer, 2004

My favorite place in the world is the cottage. Here are a few pictures of Mom and me having fun at the beach!

Another great summer at the cottage. Everybody calls me the "fishing dog." I love to catch minnows. All my friends are still at the cottage in Canada. Mickey, Minnie, Milton, Chaucer, Doogie and lots of cats that I love to chase.

January, 2005

Well, Mom had to have belly surgery again. The good thing was she got to be home for a month, but the bad thing was she had to go away for four days to get her belly fixed. I really missed her while she was gone!

March-June, 2005

Mom isn't doing very well. She tries to go to work but she doesn't feel good. In April, her Dr. told her she needed to rest and needed to be at home. She decided to do something called "retire" from work. She told me that she would be home with me all the time - what could be better than that!

June, 2005

Now it was my time to be sick. Mom noticed I was really tired and drinking lots of water. She already knew I had something called "diabetes" but she took me to see Dr. Roni to make sure. Of course, she was right. Mom is always right (don't tell Dad I said that.)

She had to learn how to give me shots in the neck to keep me healthy. I had a rough couple of months until Dr. Roni figured out how much insulin I needed every day. I don't like this shot stuff but it gives Mom & Dad another reason to spoil me.

Summer-Fall, 2005

My buddy, Ollie, isn't doing very well. He had to have hip and knee surgery again. His Mom, Connie, is really worried about him. I really miss him - we can't run and look for squirrels since he had surgery.

Mom is home all the time now since she retired. It is the best - we just hang out together all the time.

I met a man called "Mr. Sam the Walking Man" earlier this year. He walks by our fence and I say "hi" to him in the morning. Well, Mom started talking to him (oh, what a shock!) and now he comes for visits and we walk with him.

Dad took this picture of Mom and me at a park this fall.

November, 2005

My dog cousin, Cocoa, went to heaven today. He had something wrong with his kidneys. His Mom, Aunt Teresa, took real good care of him so he wouldn't be in pain. Cocoa loved bread so she soaked bagels and made them real soft and gooey so he could eat them. He got to sleep in the big bed with her and he loved it. He is now in heaven with all of our four-legged family members and Grandpa is taking care of him.

Winter, 2005-2006

Mom got my insulin under control and I'm doing much better. I don't get those dizzy spells any more. I've lost a lot of weight since Mom & Dad don't feed me a lot of junk food any more. Sometimes Dad cheats and Mom yells at him.

Spring-Summer, 2006

I love this retirement stuff - Mom is home 24/7!! And, when Dad comes home from work, I make sure that I make a big deal about him coming home. Mom and I don't want him to be jealous that we are home all day watching "The View" and "Oprah" and eating bon bons!

Welcoming Dad home from work!

The summer at the cottage is the best. Mom and I take big long walks in the woods and on the beach.

Here is a photo from this year.

Mom has started to knit scarves. Her friend, Jackie, taught her how to knit when she was sick. Her little business is called "Setter Ridge Scarfs" - of course, all about the dogs! So, when she goes to sell her stuff she puts a scarf on me and takes me with her. She said that she will share something called a "commission" with me.

November 5, 2006

My 10th Birthday!!

The day started out great - Mom spoiling me more than usual. Then, I jumped up on the bed to wake Dad up from a nap and I leaned over him and yawned.

Well, Dad spotted a black lump on the roof of my mouth - not good! Of course, Mom rushed me to the vet and the Dr. said things didn't look good. Mom tried really hard not to cry - she asked lots of questions and decided after talking to Dad that I needed to have surgery.

So, the next Monday I had to go to the dog hospital (I really don't like that place) and Dr. Mark operated on me. I was in pain so he gave me medicine to make me feel better. The lump was something called "cancer." Everybody was really upset so I'm thinking that this cancer stuff is a mean thing.

Dr. Melissa, my on-call Canadian vet, even called from another country to check on me!

December, 2006

Mom took me to a specialist who can get rid of that cancer germ and I had to have something called "radiation." It was okay - not as bad as I thought it would be. I got a little tired and sore, but I handled it. Mom & Dad always went with me for my treatments and then they took me to a park afterwards so I could run and chase ducks.

Spring, 2007

Even with all the stuff the Dr.'s did to me they told my Mom & Dad that I may not live very long and I may be going to heaven soon. Well, I showed them! Six months after surgery the Dr.'s couldn't find any cancer germs in me! The special Dr. told Mom to take me to the cottage and enjoy me!

So, that is what we did and we had an awesome summer at the cottage - the best ever!!

Here are some photos from that season at the cottage.

Here I am with my Mom on Mother's Day, 2007.

Halloween, 2007

Another Halloween - Mom made Nutmeg get dressed up this year too!!

Here we are with Dad!

November 5, 2007

My 11th birthday!! I showed all those Dr.'s how tough I am. One year surviving that darn cancer!!

Dr. Mark said he was so happy! He said that he thinks I'm healthy because of something called "Divine Intervention" - I think he means God! He also said that how much Mom & Dad spoil me might also have something to do with it - I think he is right!!

I have the best life!!

Winter, 2008

Life is pretty good. I feel good most of the time. Sometimes I choke on food from my treatments, but Mom & Dad rub my neck and help me feel better.

Mr. Sam comes over most mornings and picks up Mom & me for our walk and sometimes helps with my shots. When I was sick, he would go to church and light a candle and pray for me - what a guy!

Oh, my human cousin, Paige, does something called the "balance beam." I started saying prayers for her when she competes. She says that when I pray for her she "nails it!"

May, 2008

That cancer germ started to grow on my paw. It got really big and started to give me problems. Mom and Connie took me to see Dr. Mark. He operated on my foot and got rid of the big germ. He told my Mom that I was so good on the operating table that I almost fell asleep. Mom wants to know why I don't act like that when she and Dad give me my insulin shots.

Here I am with my foot all bandaged up.

June, 2008

Well, I had just recovered from having that thing taken off my foot, when I chased Kiki (an old black cat that lives by Ollie) and did something to my back leg. I thought Kiki was a squirrel - I would have never chased Kiki. She walks with us at Connie's house - she actually does laps around the tennis court!

Whatever happened to my leg, it hurt real bad. I never cried, but Mom knew something was wrong. Dr. Mark (my bone and bump doctor) looked at my leg and told Mom that I had torn my ACL - just like some famous golfer named, Tiger Woods. I guess he blew his ACL earlier in the week. He was chasing a golf ball - not a cat like me!

I couldn't have surgery to fix it because of my age and diabetes. My human cousin, Sydney, went with me and Mom to the vet. At the time, Sydney was only 11, but she had to be the adult at the clinic. Mom cried and was real scared and Sydney had Mom's cell phone in case she had to call someone if things got real bad.

Needless to say, it was a tough summer. I couldn't walk for very long or very far. Mom tried taking me to the cottage, but there were too many temptations. The lake, bunnies and squirrels kept getting in the way of me getting better. When Mom & Dad weren't looking, I would try and take off for the beach, but Mom always caught me.

Mom and I stayed home a lot this summer because it was too stressful for me (and Mom) at the cottage while I was recovering.

Fall, 2008

My leg is better - still weak - but I convinced Mom that I could take walks. She had a special brace made for me - she hopes Dad never asks how much it really cost!!

I don't get to do as much as I used to, but life is still great!

Here are some photos from the cottage this fall.

Halloween, 2008

I still dress up at 12 yrs. old!

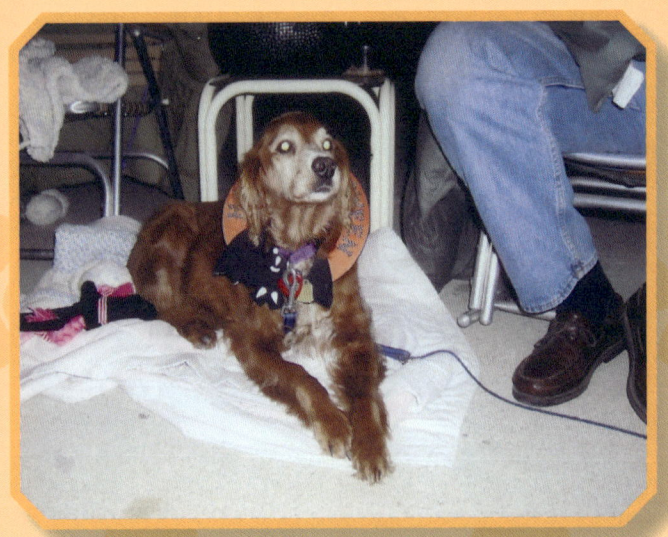

November 5, 2008

My 12th birthday!!! Hooray!

Well, I'm still here on earth. Mom & Dad made a really big deal about my birthday this year. Mom made special cards and sent them to special people. Can you believe that some people actually thought my Mom was a little crazy for doing that! Mom says she doesn't care what anyone thinks when it comes to me.

Winter, 2009

It was a very cold and snowy winter. We couldn't walk like other years - my leg would get cold and stiff. Here is a picture of Mom and me when we did go out in the cold.

Mom goes to a place called Curves to exercise. She is always worrying about her weight! They had a fundraiser for the animal shelter and everyone got to bring in photos of their pets. Mom put one up telling everyone that I'm a cancer survivor!

I found out my neighbor at home loves dogs. I go over there and she feeds me. She even makes her husband get a doggy bag when he goes out to eat just for me! If they don't know that I'm at their door, I just bark and they let me in! Had I known they love dogs so much, I would have gone over there years ago!

Here I am with my buddies at home!

March, 2009

We went to the cottage for another season, I got so excited that I started to whine and bark when I realized we were in Canada. Dad calls me his "international girl."

Everyone was real happy to see all of us together.

April-June, 2009

I haven't been doing so good. I'm skinny and I can tell my Mom is worried about me. I'm tired and started getting dizzy again. Mom talked to Dr. Roni and they adjusted my insulin. I am eating better and even have a little tummy again.

Mom & Dad are taking me for lots of walks this spring - here are pictures from this year.

Oh, that Grandma!! Months ago, she started sending mashed potatoes with cheese and stuff home for me when Mom would go visit her. They are so good I won't even share them with Dad!

July 12, 2009 - The Final Chapter

I told my Mom & Dad that I was ready to go to heaven today. They had always promised me that heaven would make me feel young again. They told me there would be no more needles, I could eat whatever I wanted and none of that darn cancer.

Mom knew the past few weeks that I was getting ready to go to heaven. She cried a lot and tried to be strong as she got ready to let me go. On that Sunday, Mom made magic and got one of my special doctors to come to our house and help me get to heaven in peace. Mom always told me she wouldn't make me go to that vet clinic and, of course, she kept her promise.

Dad gave me a hug and a kiss and told me he loved me. Mom held my face as I went to heaven on the wings of angels (that is what my human cousin, Paige, thinks happens to us dogs.) Mom told me that she would see me some day in heaven. She said my big sister, Shyloe, was waiting for me along with their other red four-legged girls. She told me not to tell them, but I was her favorite girl!! Mom said that Grandpa and Uncle Dick would be there to take care of me. I guess there is a garage where we will all hang out and I will have my own special fort. She said that Grandpa will have rules and Uncle Dick will feed me.

So, this is the end of my very spoiled life on earth and I want to thank Mom & Dad for giving me the "Life of Riley!"

EPIILOGUE

The days following Riley's death were nothing short of emotional, heartwarming and remarkable.

Friends, family and neighbors started calling and arriving at our home to offer their condolences within hours of her passing. They brought flowers, food, wine, framed pet poems, memorial pet markers and sympathy cards.

I always knew Riley was a special dog and the outpouring of kindness and sympathy that we received from everyone confirmed what a "miracle girl" she really was. With her sweet face and gentle spirit she touched the lives of so many people during her time here on earth.

LaVergne, TN USA
03 June 2010
184856LV00001B